CHILDREN'S LIT.

ANCONA

It's a baby

It's a Baby!

by George Ancona

E. P. Dutton   New York

To Pablito

Copyright © 1979 by George Ancona

Library of Congress Cataloging in Publication Data
Ancona, George.   It's a baby!
SUMMARY: Observes an infant's development during the
months between his birth and first birthday.
1. Infants–Juvenile literature.   [1. Babies]   I. Title.
HQ781.A5   1979   301.43'14   79-10453   ISBN: 0-525-32598-0

Published in the United States by E. P. Dutton, a Division
of Elsevier-Dutton Publishing Company, Inc., New York
Published simultaneously in Canada by Clarke,
Irwin & Company Limited, Toronto and Vancouver
Editor: Ann Troy   Designer: George Ancona

Printed in the U.S.A.   First Edition
10 9 8 7 6 5 4 3 2 1

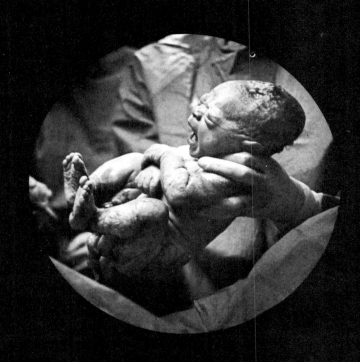

A baby is born.

It takes its first breath and cries,

telling the world it is here.

This new person is a baby boy.

His name is Pablo.

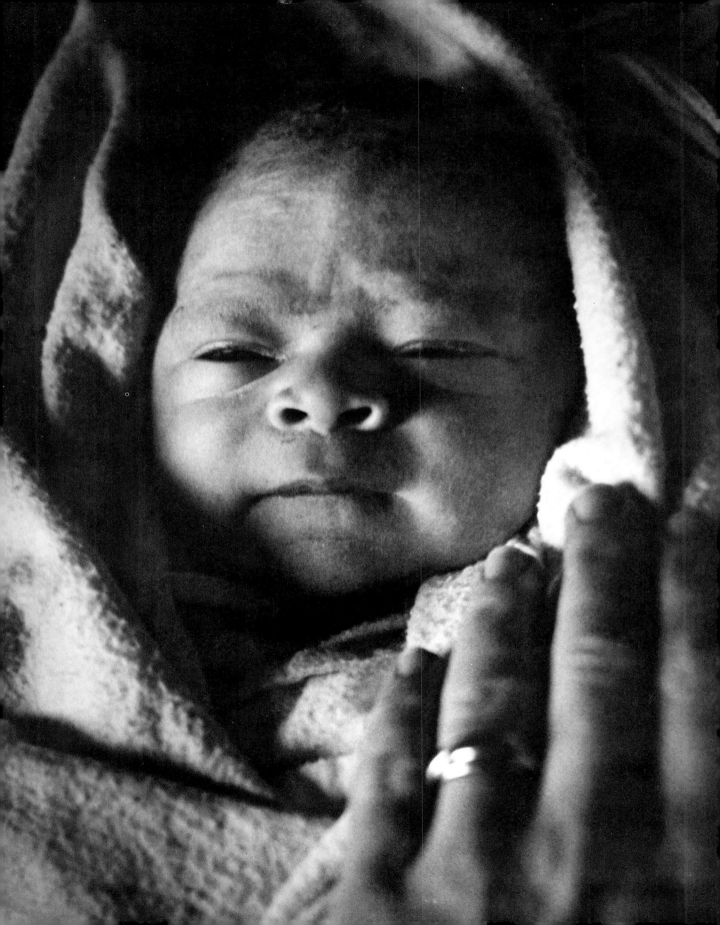

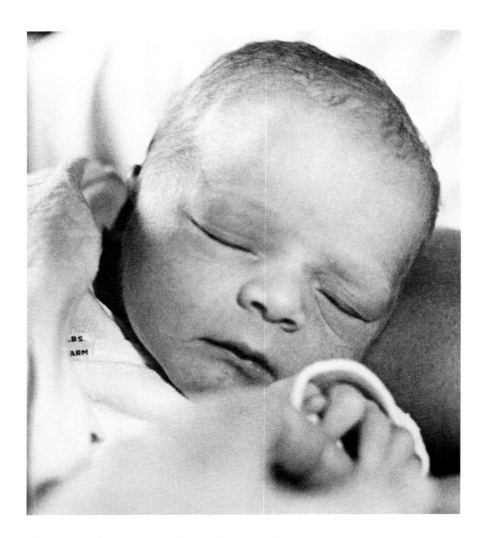

Being born is hard work.
After he is washed and wrapped in
a blanket, he falls fast asleep.

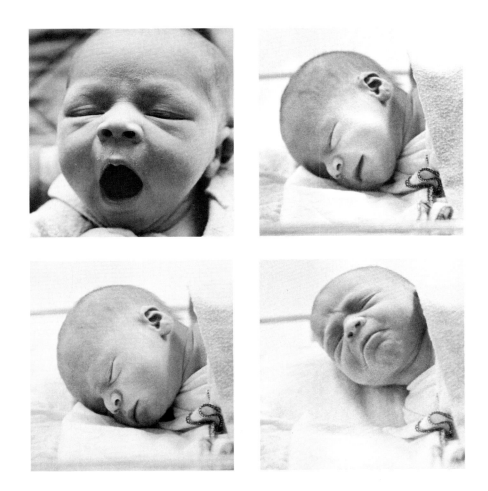

During this long sleep, the baby yawns,
smiles, squirms, and makes funny faces.
He is getting used to breathing and
to being outside his mother.

When the baby opens his eyes,
all he can see are light and dark fuzzy
shapes. But he can smell and hear.
Soon he knows his mother by her smell
and by the sound of her voice.

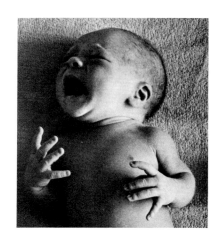

Pablo cries often.
It is his way of saying that he
wants something. Tears won't come
out until he grows a little more.

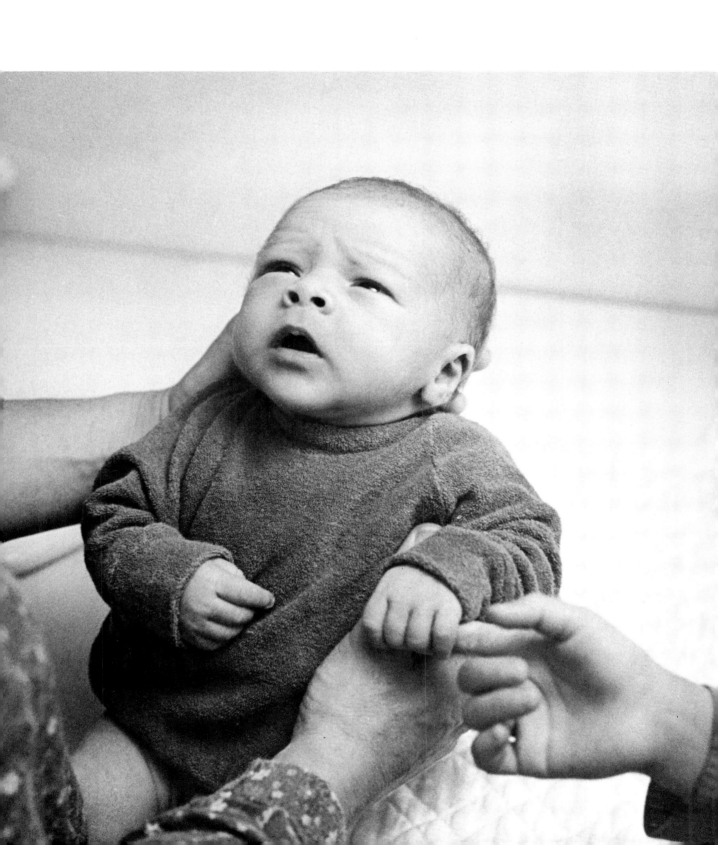

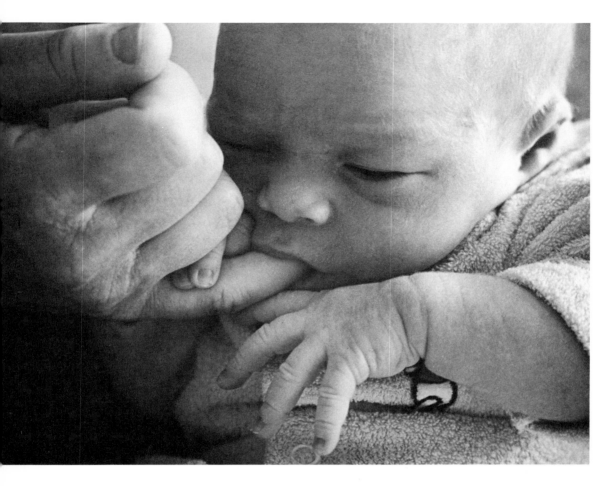

Sucking is one of the many things a newborn baby knows how to do. This is the way he gets milk from his mother's breast or from a bottle.

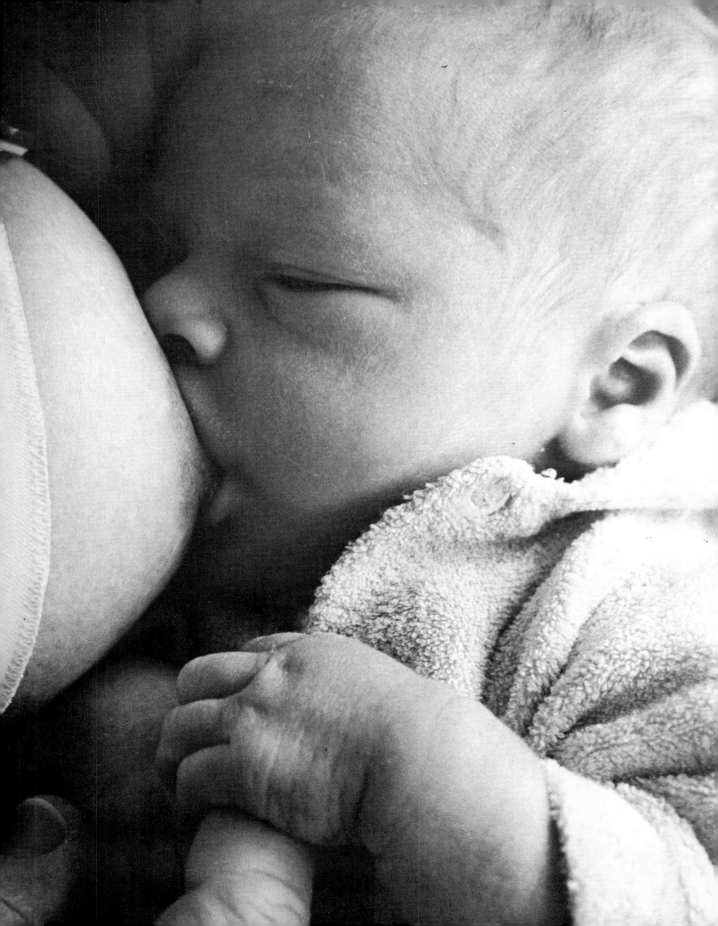

Before Pablo was born, he moved
and squirmed inside his mother. Now
he can freely move his legs.

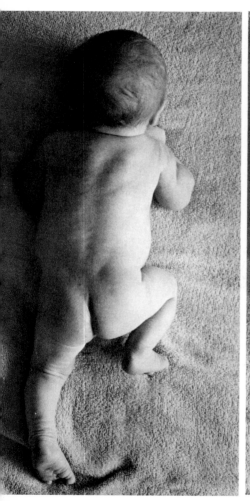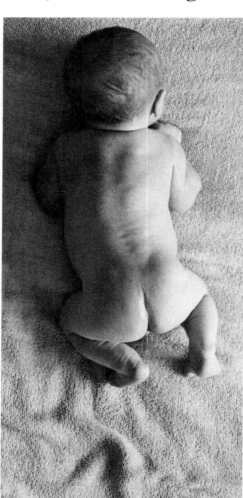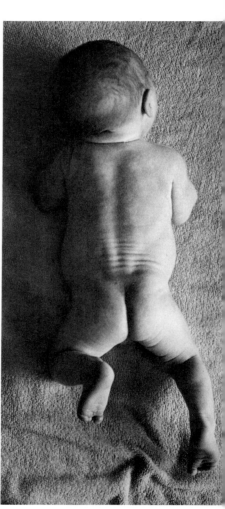

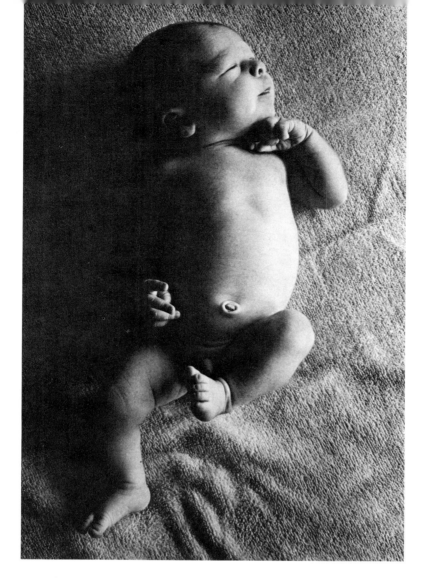

At birth, he was left with a tiny bit
of the umbilical cord on his belly.
Soon it will dry up and fall off.
It won't hurt. There he will have
a brand-new belly button.

Growing up is learning to do things for yourself. One of the first things that Pablo learns to do is to bring his hand to his mouth. This makes him happy. By using his mouth, he learns to taste, bite, and make new sounds.

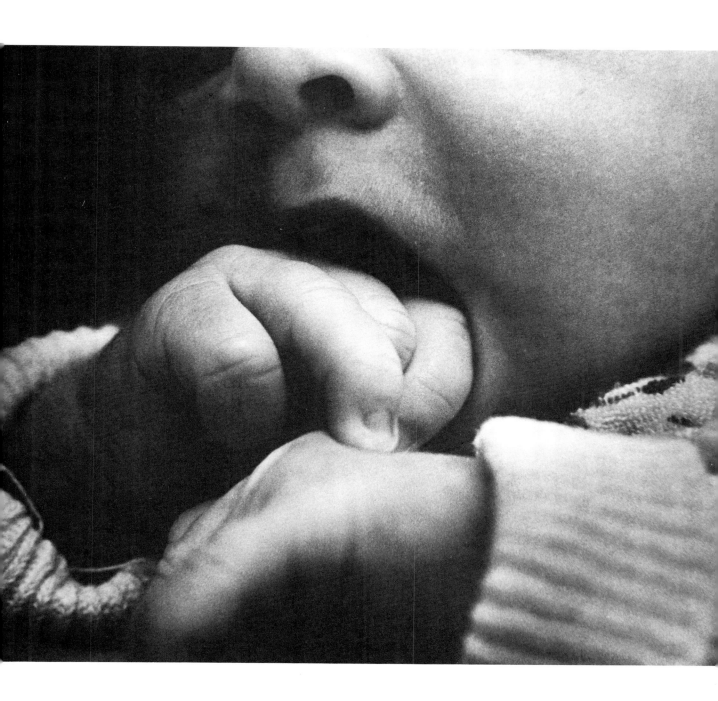

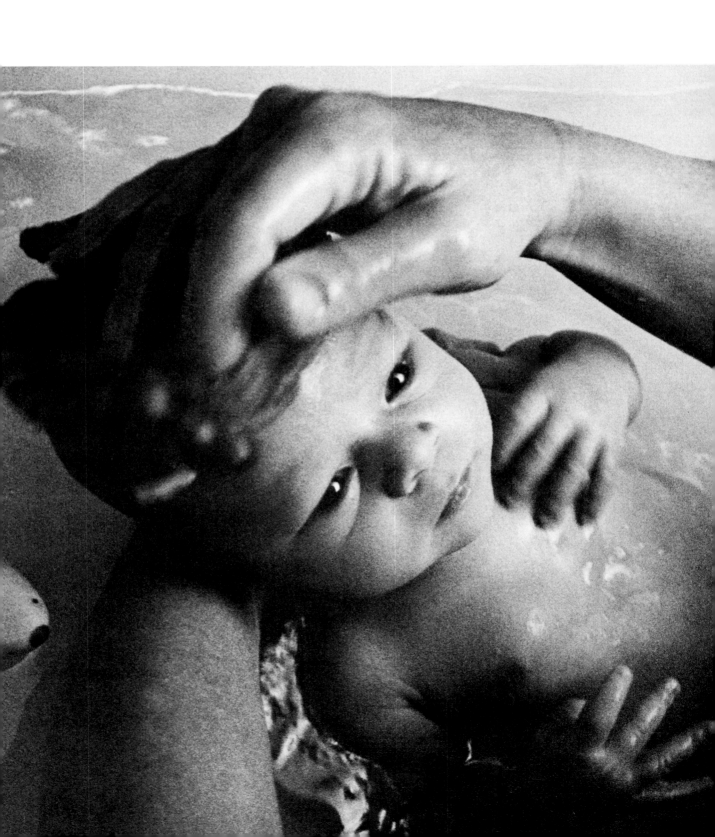

Every day, Pablo gets a bath.

He likes to kick and splash in the water.

(Don't you?)

After the bath he is patted dry and

dressed in clean clothes.

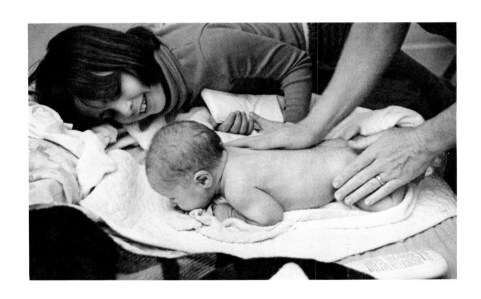

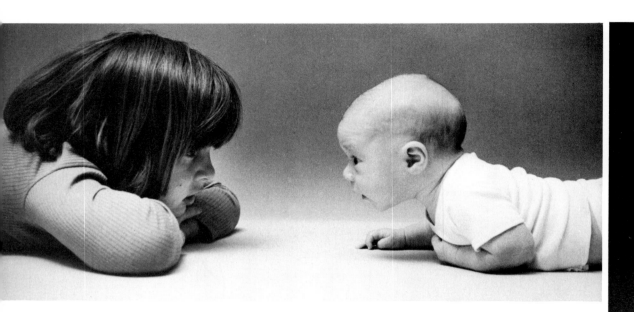

Pablo is now two months old. He can
hold up his head to look around.
He begins to see things that are
near and far.

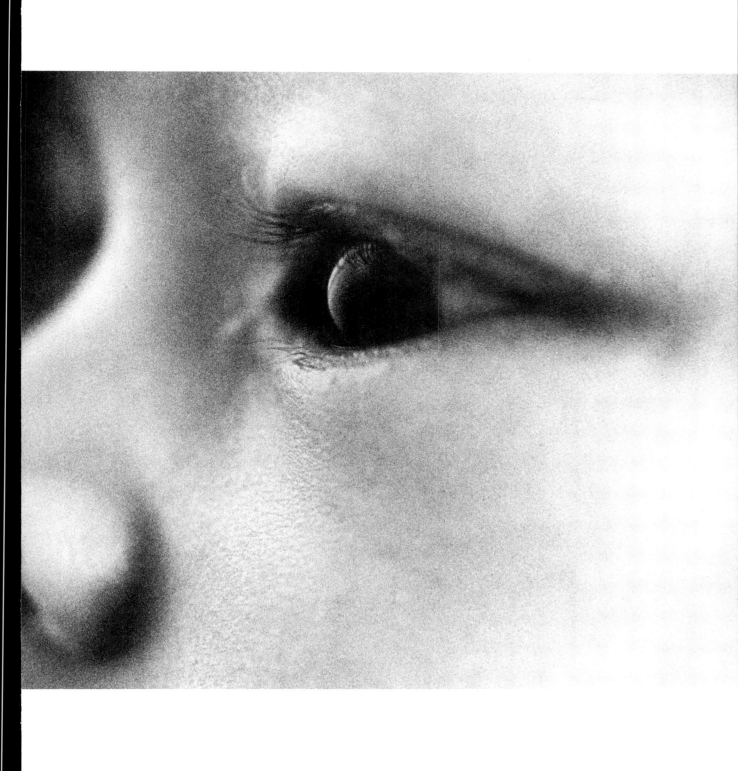

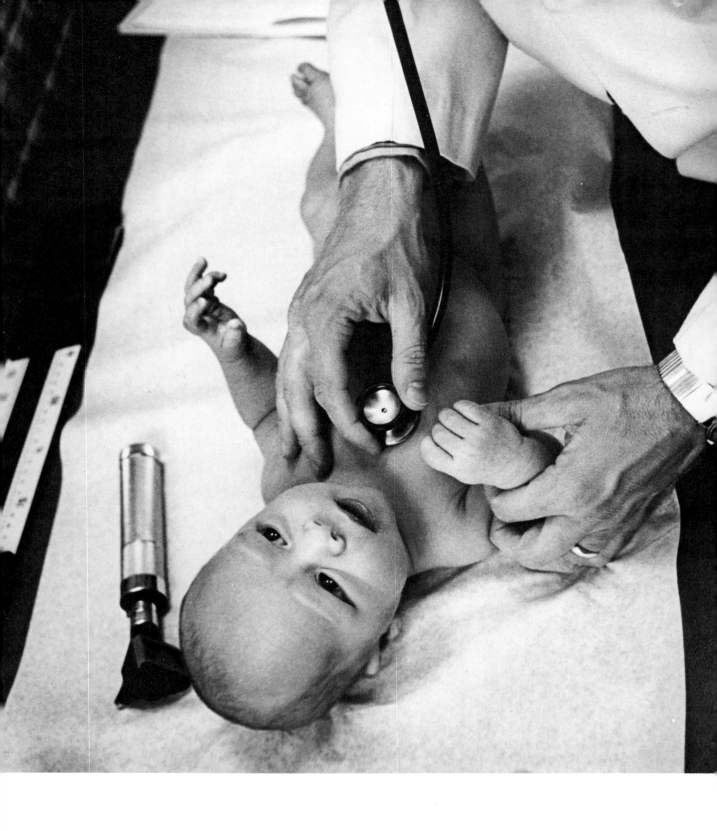

Each month, Pablo is taken to a baby doctor. A baby doctor is called a pediatrician. Pablo is examined, weighed, and measured to see how well he is growing. If he is sick, he will get medicine. Sometimes the doctor will give Pablo a shot to keep him from getting sick. This makes Pablo cry.

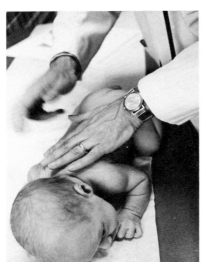

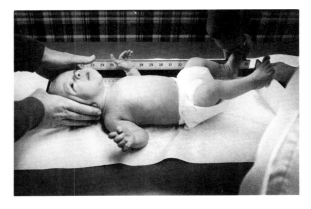

Whether the baby nurses at his mother's
breast or drinks from a bottle, he likes
to be held and cuddled. As he drinks, he
swallows air. This bothers him. Pat him on
the back, and the air comes out with
a burp. Then he can go to sleep.

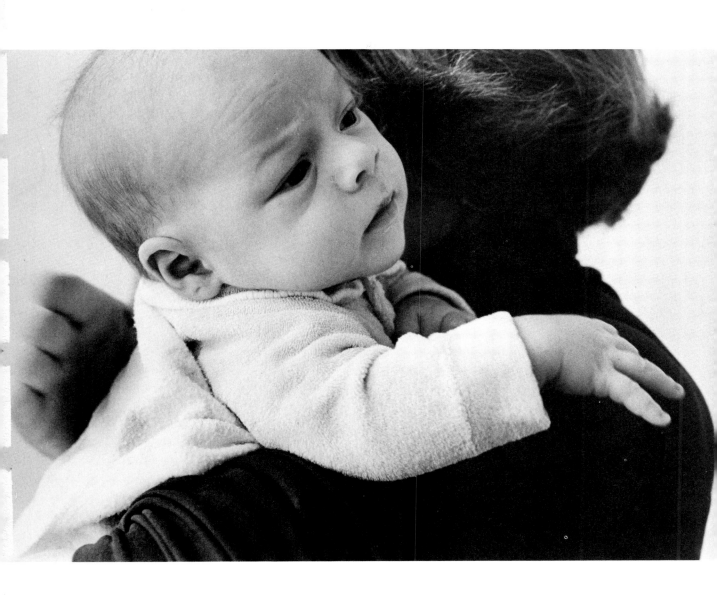

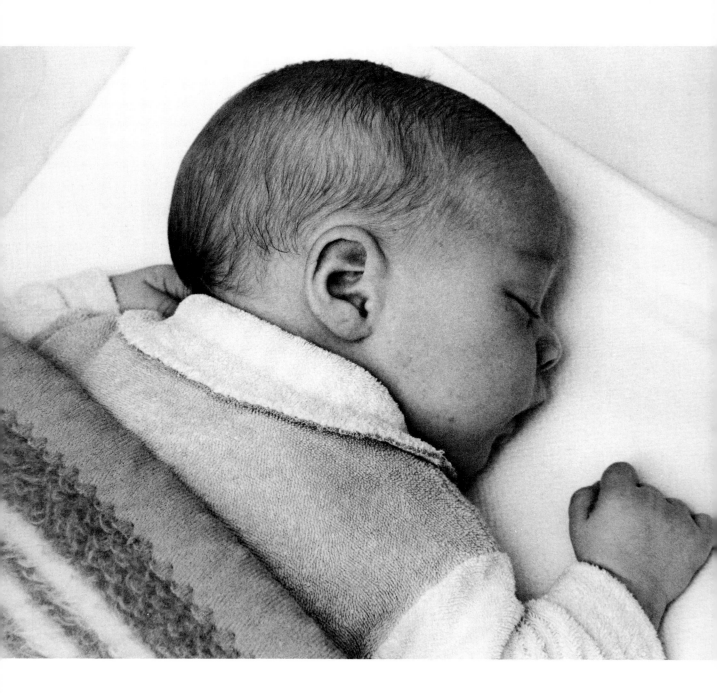

In the beginning, there was no day or night for Pablo. He would sleep and wake up at any time. Now he sleeps all night long and naps during the day.

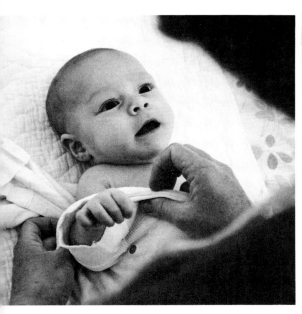

When he awakens, he looks for his mother's face. While she talks and sings to him, he answers with gurgles, coos… and smiles.

Pablo is four months old. When he is put
on his tummy, he can push himself up with
his arms. He rolls from side to side and
sometimes turns over. If someone holds
him, he can sit up.

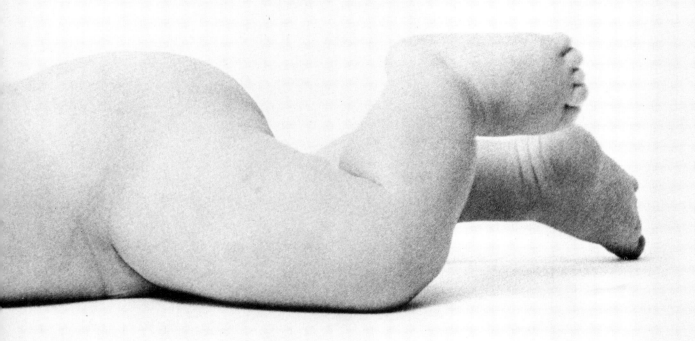

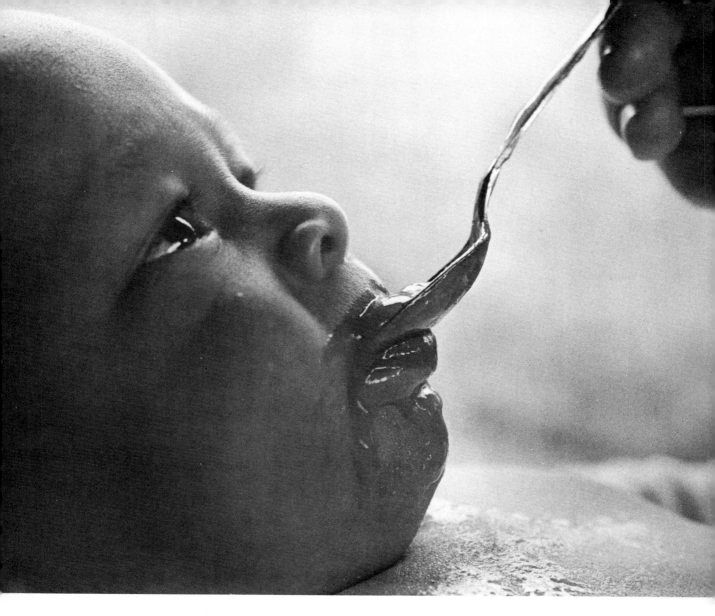

Pablo drinks milk and also eats vegetables, meat and fruit. His teeth haven't come out yet, so his food must be chopped and strained.

When he doesn't like something, he lets
you know by dribbling or spitting it out.
After he eats, his diaper may have to
be changed.

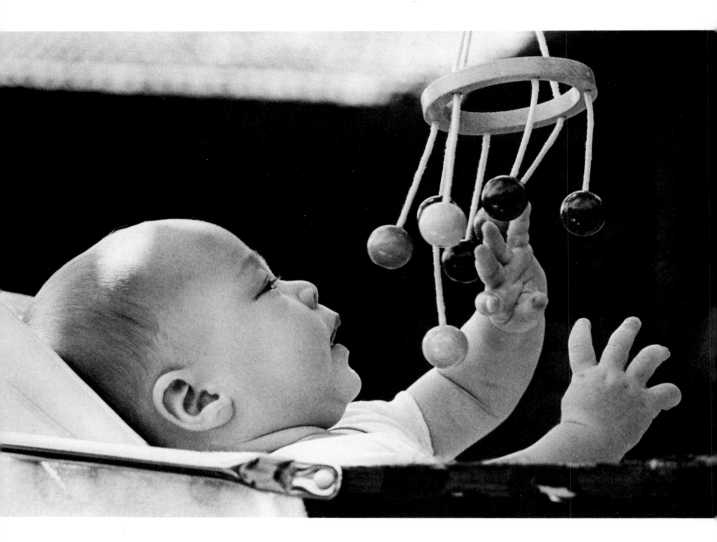

Six months have passed since Pablo was
born. Now when he sees something,
he reaches out to grab it.

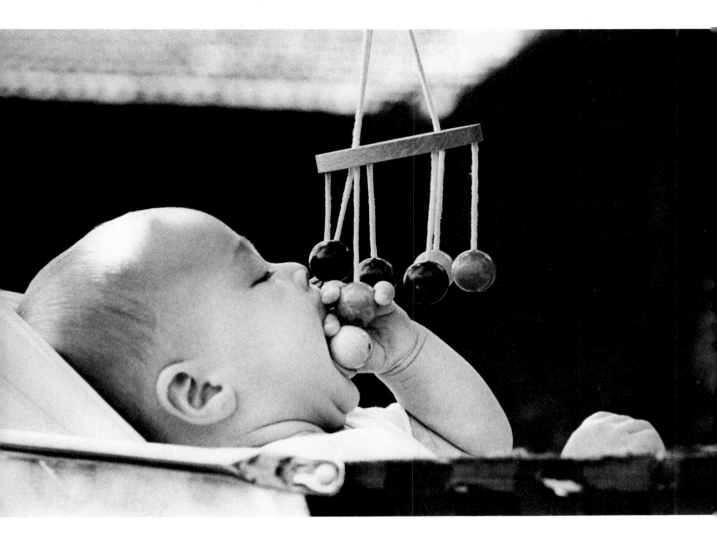

Under his gums, little teeth
are growing. Biting helps them
to come out.

When Pablo is on his belly, he flings his legs up and rolls over. He can also move around by creeping on his belly.

By this time, Pablo has learned to use
his hands and feet to move about. When he
wants to go someplace, he crawls slowly,
like a turtle.

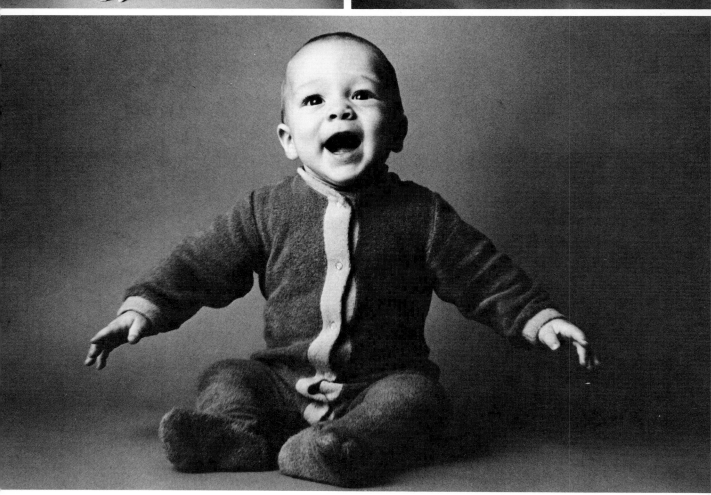

One day he stops crawling. He
pushes himself to one side and finds
that he is sitting up.

As he crawls about, Pablo discovers
stairs. Since stairs are for climbing,
that's what he does. Getting back down
is harder. He will start by crawling
backwards. He must always be watched
so he won't get hurt.

All that biting on his fingers, toys,
raw apples and carrots has helped to
bring out Pablo's teeth. Now he can bite
Daddy's nose and Grandma's finger.

When Pablo crawls to a chair, he can pull
himself up and stand. If a chair isn't
handy, a grown-up will do.

He crawls around and goes exploring,
opening and closing doors, filling and
emptying boxes, picking up and throwing
down toys... and making lots of noise.

Twelve months have gone by. It is time
to celebrate Pablo's first birthday.
Since he doesn't know about birthdays,
everyone else sings. Pablo eats cake.

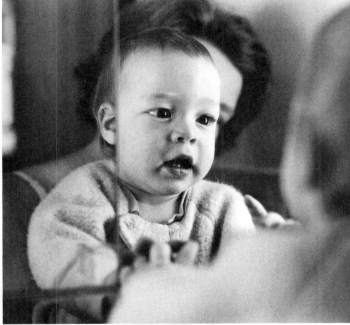

It must be a surprise to him to meet another
person his size—even in a mirror.

Shortly after his birthday, Pablo can stand up by himself. When he moves one leg in front of the other, he is walking. He falls down often, but quickly gets up to run into waiting arms…

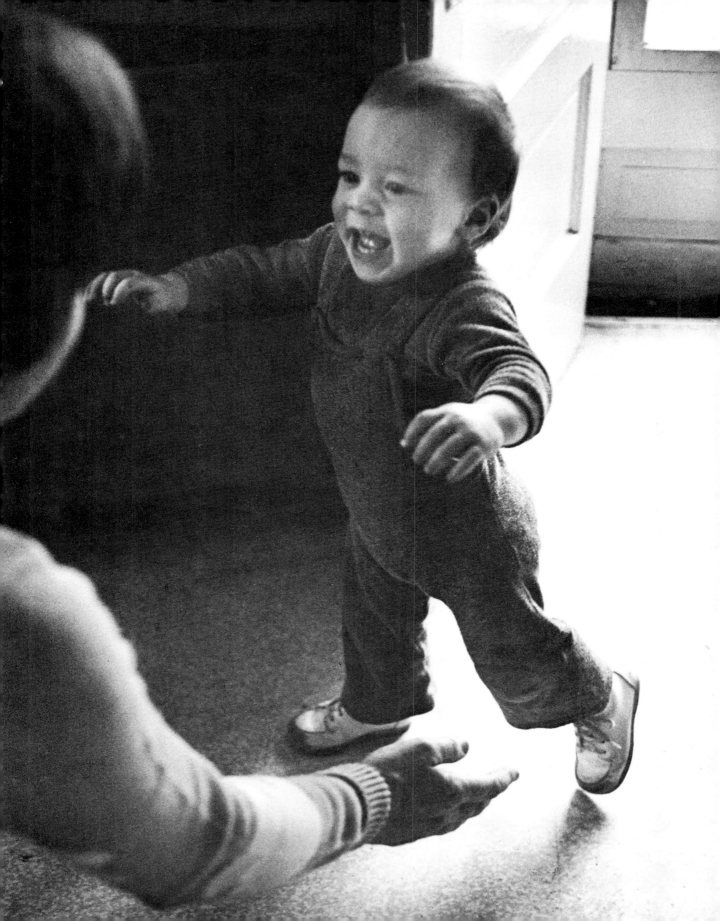

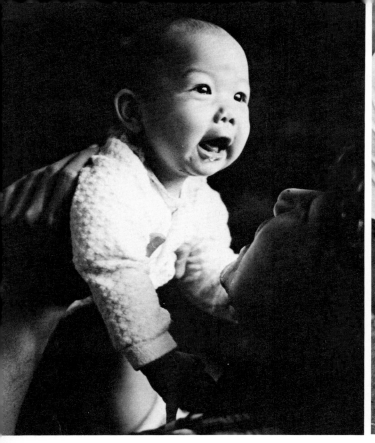

because babies are for holding,

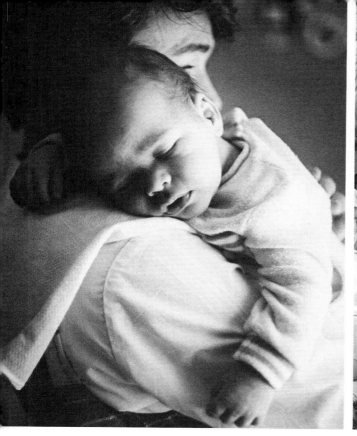

hugging,   and loving.

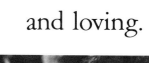

My thanks to Helga, my wife,
for giving birth to Pablo, our son.

George Ancona